PLANTS DO AMAZING THINGS!

Some plants eat insects. Some trees seem to walk. Some flowers smell bad enough to make you faint!

This carefully researched book tells about the astonishing things that different plants can do—and how and why they do them. Filled with funny facts and creepy facts and just plain interesting facts, *Plants Do Amazing Things* is an entertaining introduction to life in the plant world.

To Murray, who inspired this book
To my nephew David, whom I hope this book inspires
And to Joel, my everyday inspiration

The author and publisher wish to thank
Daphne S. Drury, former Instructor at the
Brooklyn Botanic Garden, for help in the
preparation of this book.

PLANTS
DO
AMAZING
THINGS

by HEDDA NUSSBAUM
illustrated by JOE MATHIEU

Step-Up Books —⌐_⌐— Random House
New York

Copyright © 1977 by Random House, Inc. All rights reserved under International and Pan-American Copyright Conventions. Published in the United States by Random House, Inc., New York, and simultaneously in Canada by Random House of Canada Limited, Toronto. LIBRARY OF CONGRESS CATALOGING IN PUBLICATION DATA: Nussbaum, Hedda. Plants do amazing things. (Step-up books; no. 25) SUMMARY: Describes a variety of plants with unusual characteristics including those that give off light and those that eat insects. 1. Plants—Juvenile literature. [1. Plants] I. Mathieu, Joseph, illus. II. Title. QK49.N87 581 75-36471 ISBN 0-394-83232-9 ISBN 0-394-93232-3 (lib. bdg.)
Manufactured in the United States of America   1 2 3 4 5 6 7 8 9 0

CONTENTS

The Movers

Have you ever seen a plant walk? Of course not. Plants don't walk. They stay in one place. But that does not mean that plants don't move. They DO move.

morning glories

four o'clocks

marigolds

Flowers open and close. Some close in the rain. They open again when the rain stops. Many flowers close up at night and open in the morning. Others open and close at different times.

You can tell the time by watching the flowers in a garden. Get up early one morning—at about 5:00. If you can stay awake, you will see some morning glories opening. Wait until about 8:30. You will see pumpkin flowers close and dandelions open. At 4:00 in the afternoon four o'clocks will open. Marigolds will close. Can you stay up until 10:00 at night? That is when moonflowers open. But don't wait up until they close. That will not be until noon the next day!

The leaves of plants move, too.
They move toward light. Put a house
plant by a window. Look at the plant
the next day. Its leaves will be facing
the window. Turn the plant around
so that the leaves face you. The
next day the leaves will be facing
the window again. The leaves moved
toward the light—by themselves.

Some leaves do a lot of moving. The leaves of the Sensitive Plant close up when anything touches them. The leaves of the clover plant fold together at night. The telegraph

plant keeps moving all day long. Its leaves grow in sets of three. Two of the leaves move up and down during the day. They seem to be sending signals. At night the leaves droop.

Who ever said that plants don't move!

The Glowers

Some plants glow in the dark. They give off light—like little electric light bulbs. These plants shine in the daylight, too. But then we cannot see them do it.

Some glowing plants shine with a green light. Some shine with an orange light. And some shine with a yellow light.

Which plants glow? Many mushrooms do. Some very tiny plants that live on dead wood do. And many, many plants that live at the bottom of the ocean glow, too.

No one knows why these plants glow. Some scientists think that glowing helps the plants keep alive. Others say that glowing helped the plants a long time ago, but that it no longer does.

Would you like to see some glowers? You can sometimes see them in the woods at night. Look for little patches of pale light glowing in the dark. The plants' light is strange and beautiful. People call this light "fox-fire."

The Food Factories

How do people get their food? They grow it. Or they hunt it. Or they buy it at the store. How do other animals get their food? They find it growing. Or they catch it and kill it. How do plants get their food? Most of them make it themselves. Green plants are very lucky. They can make their food right in their own leaves. Their leaves are like little food factories.

Each leaf factory needs three things to make food. First, it needs a gas called carbon dioxide (die-OCK-side). There is plenty of this gas in the air. A leaf takes the carbon dioxide right from the air.

Second, the leaf factory needs water. When rain falls, it soaks into the earth. A plant's roots bring the rain water up from the earth. The water travels through the plant to the leaves.

Now the leaf factory is almost ready to make food. It needs one more thing. It needs something to make the factory work.

A car needs gasoline to make it work. A toaster needs electricity. A leaf factory needs sunlight. When sunlight hits a green leaf, the factory starts to work. When the sun goes down, the factory stops.

A real factory gives off smoke while it is working. A leaf factory gives off a gas called oxygen (OCK-sih-jin). Smoke dirties the air. But oxygen does not. In fact, animals need this oxygen to live. If they don't have oxygen to breathe, they die.

The food that the leaf factory makes is sugar. The plant uses the sugar for energy. It must have energy to live and grow.

Sometimes the plant makes more food than it can use. So it stores some in its roots, seeds, stems, and fruit. The plant uses the stored food whenever there is no sunlight for making new food.

Guess who sometimes eats the stored food? You do. And so do other animals. The potatoes and carrots that you eat hold food made by plants. So do peas and green beans. So do blueberries and apples.

When you eat this food, you get energy. When other animals eat this food, they get energy. When you eat the meat of the other animals, you get more energy. What would you do without plants!

The Traders

Lichens (LIE-kinz) do not look like most plants. They have no leaves. They have no flowers. Some look like crusty spots of gray, green, or orange. Some look like little green wineglasses. Others look like feathery gray beards. They live on rocks and trees and sand and dead wood. They grow in the hottest deserts and on the coldest mountains. You can find lichens almost anywhere but in cities. The dirt in city air kills them.

What are these odd plants? Lichens are two-in-one plants. They are made up of two kinds of tiny plants that live together. One kind is called algae (AL-jee). The other is fungi (FUN-ji). Each kind of plant helps the other to live.

The algae are green plants. They make their own food. They need water to do it. But they don't have any roots to take in water.

The fungi are not green plants. They cannot make food. They don't have any roots to take in water, either. But they can take water right from the air. So they make a trade with the algae.

The fungi take water from the air. They give some to the algae. In return, the algae make food and give some to the fungi.

Because the algae and fungi trade this way, lichens can live where no other plants can.

They can live where there is no soil. Neither algae nor fungi could live there alone. The fungi would starve. The algae would dry out.

Lichens are very small. But they do a big job. Those that live on rocks can help to make soil. They give off a liquid that slowly crumbles the rock. When lichens die, they mix with the crumbled rock. Soil is formed. Then other plants can grow there. First come some other plants with no flowers— mosses and ferns. Later, plants with flowers can move in, too. Bare spots become living spots—thanks to the lichens.

The Meat Eaters

You may have heard stories of giant man-eating plants. They catch people in the jungle. They eat the people alive. Well, THERE ARE NO SUCH PLANTS!

Some plants do eat meat. But they are much too small to eat people. A few of them eat mice and small birds. But most cannot eat anything bigger than an insect.

Why do meat eaters eat meat? They are all green plants. They can make their own food. And they do. But plants need more things than food to stay healthy. They need minerals (MIN-er-ulz) and nitrogen (NIE-tro-jin), too. These come from the soil. They are mixed in the water that the roots take in. Meat-eating plants live in poor soil. It does not have enough minerals and nitrogen. But meat has these things in it. So the plants get the extra things they need by eating meat.

Many meat eaters grow in wet places in the United States. So keep your eyes open for sundews, bladderworts, Venus flytraps, and pitcher plants.

A sundew has many little hairs on its leaves. At the end of each hair is a tiny drop of liquid. It is sweet and sticky. When the sun shines on the plant, the liquid shines like dew.

Insects are attracted
to the shining drops and
the sweet smell. An insect
lands on a leaf. It gets
stuck in the sticky liquid.
The nearby hairs bend over
it. They hold the insect down.
It cannot escape. What a nasty trick!

The plant then puts out a digestive
(die-JEST-iv) juice. This juice kills the insect
and makes it soft. Now the sundew can take
what it needs from the insect. It digests the
insect in the same way that your stomach
digests food. Some parts of the insect are not
needed. They fall off the plant later.

Sometimes a twig or a pebble falls on a
sundew leaf. The leaf hairs barely move. The
sundew does not put out any digestive juice.
It seems to know what it can eat.

Fish and water insects, beware! The traps of the bladderwort plant may get you! Many bladderworts live in ponds. Their leaves are underwater. Attached to the leaves are little hollow balls. These are called bladders. They catch and digest the victims. Some bladders are so small, you need a magnifying glass to see them.

Each bladder has a trap door. Near the trap door are little hairs. Sometimes a water insect or tiny fish swims by. It touches some of the hairs. That signals the bladder. Slurp! It quickly sucks the victim in through the trap door. The door closes behind. The victim has no way out. Most of it gets eaten. The bladder spits out the leftovers. Then it is ready for its next meal.

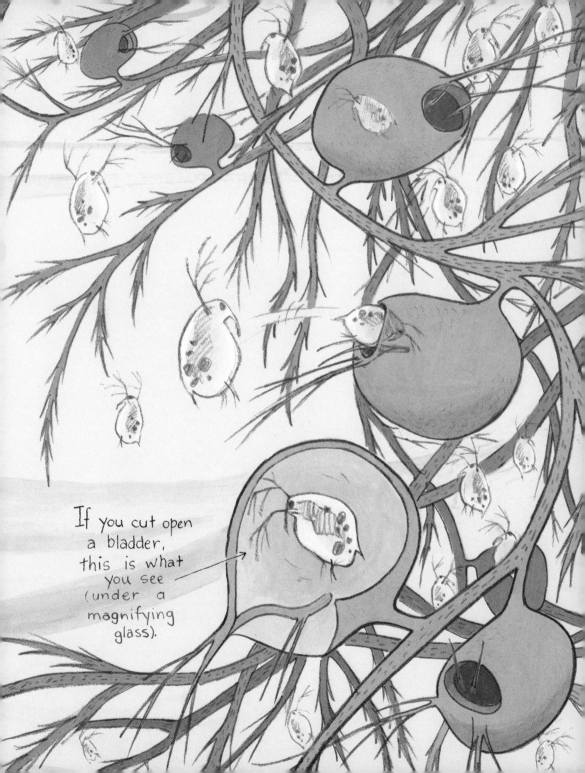

If you cut open
a bladder,
this is what
you see
(under a
magnifying
glass).

Can the Venus flytrap count? It seems to. On each of its leaves are six hairs. If one of the hairs is touched one time, nothing happens. If two of the hairs are touched one time, the leaf folds in half. If one hair is touched two times, the leaf folds in half. The number two is the signal for the leaf to close like a trap.

When a raindrop falls on the trap, it touches only one hair, one time. The leaf does not close. A good thing! Once a leaf closes, it may not open for a whole day. So it must not close on anything but a meal. If the leaf kept closing on the wrong things, it might never get a chance to eat.

An insect usually moves around when it lands on a leaf. The leaf gets the "two signal"—and closes fast! Long spikes on each side of the leaf lock together. The insect is trapped inside. Slowly the leaf will digest it.

Pitcher plants have leaves shaped like vases. Along the rim of each leaf is a sweet liquid. The liquid attracts insects. They crawl or fall inside. Once inside, an insect cannot crawl out. The sides of the leaf are too slippery. The insect falls to the bottom.

At the bottom of the leaf is water. It is mixed with digestive juices. The insect drowns. It is then digested by the plant. Yummy!

If you cut a pitcher in half, this is what you see.

The Thirsty One

In the desert grows a tall green plant. It is ten times taller than you are. But this plant is not a tree. It has no bark. It has no wood. It has no leaves. The plant makes food in its green stem. It is covered with sharp spines.

This plant is the saguaro (sah-GWAH-row) cactus. It is the largest cactus in the world. Sometimes it grows to be 50 feet tall.

The saguaro can bloom and grow fruit for years with almost no rain. But it gets very thirsty. After a big rain, it can drink up to one-half ton of water from the earth. Some saguaros drink so much that they burst!

Most saguaros do not burst when they drink. The cactus can hold a lot of water because its sides can stretch. A very large saguaro can hold almost ten tons of water. The cactus stores the water to use in dry months. As it uses up the water, its sides slowly tighten up again.

A saguaro is often a woodpecker's home. Woodpeckers make holes in the cactus and build their nests inside. Why doesn't the water pour out when a hole is made? The water has become a part of the plant's body. The insides of the cactus look something like the white of a watermelon.

Can you eat the saguaro? Some Arizona Indians do. They make jam and syrup from its fruit. But don't look for saguaro jam at your local supermarket!

The Stranglers

Some trees are stranglers! But don't worry. They won't harm you—unless you are another tree.

The strangler fig is one kind of strangler tree. It grows in hot, damp places like Florida. No one knows why, but its seeds will not grow in the ground. They will grow only on another tree. The other tree is called a host tree.

Birds like to eat the strangler fig's seeds. Sometimes a bird drops a seed in a crack on another tree. The crack may be very high up on a branch. It may be very low down on the trunk. Wherever the crack is, the seed starts to grow in it.

The seed grows a stem and roots. The roots grow in the air, along the trunk of the host tree. They take water right from the air.

Some of the roots grow straight down the trunk. After a long time, they reach the ground. They push deep inside the earth. Then they bring water up from underground—just as most roots do. The part of each root that is still above the ground gets thick and woody. It looks like a little tree trunk. People call it a prop root.

Some of the strangler fig's roots never reach the ground. Instead, they grow in a circle around the trunk of the host tree. They grow thick and woody, too. They join together wherever they touch. They press tighter and tighter against the host. The host's trunk cannot grow. Little by little the roots strangle the host tree.

While the roots are growing from the seed, the stem is growing, too.

Branches grow out of it.
The branches reach very
high. They may grow higher
than the host tree. If so, their
leaves block the light from
the host tree. The poor host!
Without sunlight it cannot
make food in its leaves.

The host slowly dies. It
is strangled and starved
to death. After a long
time, it rots away. The
strangler roots of the
fig tree are left
growing around
an empty space.

Another tree that can be a strangler is the banyan (BAN-yun). Its seeds can grow in soil. But it sometimes starts life in another tree. Then it acts just like the strangler fig.

The banyan does one other amazing thing. It keeps sending down new roots from its branches. These roots turn into very thick prop roots. Each one may grow up to eight feet thick!

The banyan's branches keep growing longer and longer. Year after year, new prop roots grow from the branches. In this way, the banyan spreads and spreads and spreads.

Up to 350 prop roots may grow on one banyan tree. In India, whole market places are built under one banyan. And people say that an army of 7,000 men once camped under one of these trees. What a great place for a school picnic!

The Seed Makers

Next time you see a honey bee on a flower, don't run away. Watch the bee. Something amazing is going on. The bee is helping the flower to make seeds. Seeds are needed so new plants can grow. But the flower can't make seeds by itself. It needs the bee's help.

The bee comes to the flower because she wants food. First she wants a sweet liquid called nectar. Nectar is in tiny cups in the flower. The bee will make honey with the nectar.

The bee wants another kind of food, too. She wants pollen. Pollen looks like yellow dust. It comes from little spikes in the center of the flower. The spikes are called stamens (STAY-minz). Each stamen has a knob at the top. The knob holds a lot of pollen. The bee collects the pollen on her back legs. Grains of pollen get all over her body, too.

But what does pollen have to do with seeds? The flower needs pollen in order to make seeds. But not just any pollen will do. The flower needs pollen from another flower of the same kind. How does it get this pollen? From the bee!

The bee flies from flower
to flower gathering pollen. She
gathers pollen from only one
kind of flower at a time. Each
time she lands on a flower, some
pollen gets brushed off her body. If the
pollen brushes off on the right place, seeds
will grow in the flower.

The right place is the pistil. This is
another spike that grows in the center of the
flower. Sometimes a flower has more than
one pistil. A pistil looks different from the
stamens. Usually it is taller or shorter. And
it is sticky. Pollen grains are sticky, too.
When they touch a pistil, they stick.

pollen
grains
on
pistil

stamens
with
pollen

a
flower
cut
in
half

When the bee puts pollen on a pistil, we say
she "pollinates" the flower. Now seeds will
grow deep inside the pistil. Soon the flower
petals will fall off. Later on, the seeds will fall
to the ground, and new plants will grow.
The flower has done its job—with the help
of the bee.

Made For Each Other

"Kerchoo!" Someone sneezes.
"It's my hay fever," he says. "There
must be a lot of pollen in the air today."

What is pollen doing in the air? The wind is
carrying it from one flower to another. Bees
are not the only ones that pollinate flowers.
The wind sometimes does it, too. So do
butterflies and moths and other insects. So
do birds and even bats. They all pollinate
different flowers. And the flowers that they
pollinate seem to be made just for them.

Some flowers attract bees. A "bee" flower
has a sweet smell that bees like. The flower is
often purple, blue, yellow, or white. Bees can
see these colors well. Some bee flowers have
colored spots close to the nectar and pollen.
The spots help the bees find their food.

A "moth" flower is long and thin.
Nectar is deep inside it. Moths have a
long tongue that can reach the nectar.
A moth flower opens at night when
moths are awake. It gives out a strong,
sweet smell. It is pale yellow or
white. Moths can see it and
smell it in the dark.

Bats love nectar and
pollen. "Bat" flowers
have a lot of both. They are
often big flowers. The bat's head
can easily fit inside. A bat flower
has a strange smell. Only bats like it.
Bat flowers do not need to have bright
colors. Bats cannot see very well.

A "bird" flower is
often bright red or orange.
It has very little smell. Birds are
attracted by bright colors, not by
smell. Bird flowers have nectar inside deep
tubes. A bird's bill fits right in the tube.

Some flowers don't need to attract anyone.
These are the flowers that are pollinated by
the wind. They have no nectar. They have no
smell. They have no bright colors. They just
have pollen. The wind carries it to other
flowers of the same kind. The wind does a
good job, too. These flowers always grow
plenty of seeds. Many "wind" flowers are in
the grass family, and you can find grass
almost everywhere!

The Good Friends

The yucca (YUCK-uh) plant and the yucca moth cannot live without each other. The plant can be pollinated only by this one moth. The moth can start its life only inside a yucca flower.

In summer the yucca
plant blooms in the
desert. The white flowers
open at night. The white
female yucca moth flies
to a flower. She gathers
pollen. She shapes the
pollen into a big ball.
The ball is bigger than
her head! She carries
it under her "chin" to
another yucca flower.

The moth makes a
hole in this flower's
pistil. She lays her eggs
deep inside it.

This is
what you see
if you cut
the pistil open.

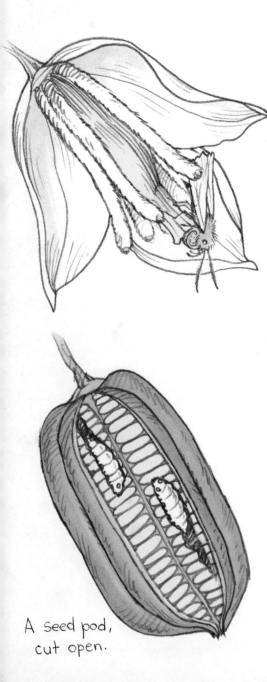

A seed pod, cut open.

The moth then puts the ball of pollen on the top of the pistil. She pollinates the yucca flower. Seeds begin to grow right next to her eggs. The pistil turns into a seed pod.

The moth's eggs hatch in four days. Little caterpillars come out and begin to eat the seeds. But they do not eat all of them. There are too many. Some seeds are left, so new plants can grow.

The caterpillars grow big and strong. Soon they are ready to leave the yucca plant. They make a hole in the wall of the seed pod. Then they spin a thread, like a spider. They use the thread to lower themselves to the ground.

The caterpillars then bury themselves. They stay in the ground almost a year. During the winter their bodies change. The caterpillars turn into moths. They leave the ground in early summer. Soon the yucca plants bloom. The new female moths lay their eggs in the yucca flowers. And the story starts all over again!

The Exploding Flowers

Exploding flowers? Can it be? Yes. Scotch broom has flowers that explode.

Each flower has five petals. Three of them stay closed up. They form a kind of envelope. Inside the envelope are the stamens and the pistil—waiting to explode.

When a light-weight ant crawls across the flower, nothing happens. When a light-weight fly lands on the flower, nothing happens. But when a heavy bee lands on the flower, it pushes open the envelope. Poof! Five stamens pop out and pour pollen all over the bee's belly. Then the pistil and more stamens pop out. The stamens curl around until they touch the bee's back. They pin the bee down for a moment. They powder the bee with more pollen.

When bumblebees are pollinating Scotch broom, they move very fast. They set off explosion after explosion. The air is filled with little pollen clouds. You might think you were seeing a battlefield full of smoke!

The Trickster

The bucket orchid (OR-kid) plays a dirty trick on bees. And in return, the bees pollinate the orchid. Here is how it all happens.

The bucket orchid opens in the morning. For a short time it gives out a delicious smell. A certain kind of male bee loves this smell. The bees swarm to the orchid. They land on it. No one is sure why, but the bees soon begin to act drunk. They bump into each other. One bee loses his balance. He slips and falls inside the flower.

A bucket
orchid cut
in half.

pollen

At the bottom
of the flower is a
liquid made by the
orchid. Splash! The
bee lands right in it.
He wants to get out—fast!
Suddenly he sees an escape
hole. He squeezes through it. As
he goes through the hole, his back gets
covered with pollen. Then he flies away.

Has the bee learned his lesson? No. The
next day he will fall into the trap of another
bucket orchid. There he will leave some
pollen from the first orchid. And he will pick
up some new pollen.

What does the bee get out of all of this?
Nectar? No. Pollen for food? No. Only a good
dunking!

The Old-timers

Eat an apple. Save the seeds. If you plant them today, they will grow. But what if you plant them a year from now? Will they still grow? Will they grow after ten years? A hundred years? A thousand years?

Most seeds will grow after a year. Many will grow after five or six years. But not longer. After that they will die.

Yet a 2,000-year-old lotus seed was planted, and it grew! Scientists knew the age of the seed because they tested it. They were very surprised to see it grow.

Some Arctic lupine (LOO-pin) seeds gave scientists an even bigger surprise. The seeds were 10,000 years old. A man found them in a deep hole in northern Canada. The hole had been covered with earth. The earth had frozen long ago. The seeds froze, too. The freezing kept them alive.

The scientists planted the seeds. Some began to grow in only two days. The plants kept on growing for years.

Just think—those plants had parents that lived 10,000 years ago!

The Giants

Have you ever picked a flower that weighed 25 pounds? "No flower weighs 25 pounds!" you say. Well, you are wrong. Deep in the jungles of an island called Sumatra grows the rafflesia (rah-FLEE-zee-uh). This plant has the largest flower in the world. The flower may weigh 15 to 25 pounds. It may be as big as four feet across. Its dark red petals are almost an inch thick.

You can hardly see the rafflesia before the flower grows on it. The plant lives mostly underground. It takes its food from the roots of another plant. The rafflesia has no leaves or stem. But when it blooms, you certainly can see it!

In the same jungles of Sumatra lives another giant—the krubi (CREW-bee). Its flower sometimes grows more than nine feet tall and four feet wide!

This is NOT the biggest flower in the world. That is because it is not just one flower. It is really thousands of tiny flowers growing together on one plant. These flowers grow at the bottom of a tall spike. A large leaf is wrapped around them. So you cannot see them.

Once some men from England found one of these giants. They wanted to take it home. So they tied it to a pole. Two men had to carry the pole. The whole plant weighed more than 100 pounds!

You probably would like to see a krubi. Well, you may soon change your mind. The flowers smell terrible—like rotting fish.

People have fainted from the smell when the plant was grown indoors.

There is a very good reason for this bad smell. It attracts the beetles that pollinate the flowers. The rafflesia smells rotten, too. Its smell attracts the flies that pollinate it. Be glad that no one has made rafflesia or krubi perfume!

The Trees That Walk

Trees that walk? How can that be? Trees can't walk! Trees have roots that keep them in one place. Yet people call mangroves "the trees that walk." Here is why.

Mangrove trees grow in Florida at the edge of the sea. They live in shallow salt water. A mangrove has odd-looking prop roots. They start above the water. They grow sideways into the air. Then they curve down through the water and into the mud. The roots look like giant spider legs. They are smooth and slippery. If you tried to walk on them, you would fall off.

The mangrove blooms all year. There are always seeds on the branches. Each seed grows a root while it is still on the tree. The root can be as long as one foot. Then the seed drops off the tree into the water.

A fallen seed may float away. Or its root may sink into the mud next to the parent tree. Then a new tree starts to grow. It grows quickly. Every hour it grows one inch! It grows a stem and branches. And it grows spidery prop roots from its stem.

More seeds drop off the parent tree. More mangrove trees begin to grow. They all have spidery roots curving out into the water.

The roots of the trees tangle in each other. Sand and bits of dirt get trapped between the roots. Soil builds up under the trees. Finally the mangroves are no longer in the water. They are on land—on a swampy island.

New mangroves keep growing up at the edge of the island. New spidery roots keep "walking" out toward the sea. Many seeds float away from the island. They root in other shallow spots and start new mangrove islands. The trees never stop spreading.

Now you can see why mangroves are called "the trees that walk"!

The Ant Lovers

Ants are pests! Who needs them? Bullhorn acacia (uh-KAY-shuh) trees do.

These trees live in Mexican forests full of plants, insects, and animals. Many plants try to crowd out the bullhorn acacias. Many insects and animals try to eat the bullhorn acacias. But something stops them. What? Ants.

If you cut open an acacia thorn, this is what you see.

Certain ants live in the bullhorn acacia's thorns. The tree makes nectar that the ants eat. In exchange, the ants protect the tree.

The ants sting insects and animals that try to eat the acacia. And they bite off the tips of any plant that grows too near.

When the bullhorn acacias have ants to protect them they grow well. But if the ants are killed off, the trees die. No wonder bullhorn acacias need ants!

The Listeners

Do you ever talk to your house plants? Many people do. They say that talking helps the plants to grow better. Is this true? Maybe. Maybe not.

Scientists are trying to find out if plants react to people. They attach a machine to a plant. Then they talk near the plant. If the plant does not react, the machine makes a mark like this: ξ . If the plant reacts strongly, the machine makes a mark like this: ⌇ . Some scientists never get any reaction to their words. Other scientists say they do. They say the plant even reacts to their thoughts. If they think nasty thoughts, the machine makes a very strong mark!

Some scientists say that plants react to music. They grow better when classical music is played all day. They die when rock music is played all the time. Why? Can they hear it? The scientists say no. But in some way the plants can feel the music. People are still trying to find out if this is true.

The other questions are still open, too. Do plants have feelings the way people do? Do they grow better when you talk to them? Do they know what you are thinking? Why not ask your plants!

ABOUT THE AUTHOR AND ILLUSTRATOR

 **Hedda Nussbaum** loves plants—both her apartment and her office are filled with them. She belongs to The New York Botanical Garden and The New York Horticultural Society. When not tending her plants, Ms. Nussbaum works as a children's book editor. Previously, she was an elementary school teacher and a textbook editor. She was born in New York City and lives there still.

 **Joe Mathieu** is a busy illustrator of books for children. Among his popular titles are *Grover and the Everything in the Whole Wide World Museum* (a Sesame Street book) and *The Giant Book of Strange But True Sports Stories.* He both wrote and illustrated *Big Joe's Trailer Truck.* He has also designed T-shirts and bed sheets. Mr. Mathieu lives in Putnam, Connecticut, with his wife and two children.